Animals and More Animals
third edition

Grandma Goes to
South Africa series

Linda L. Sheehan

ISBN-13: 978-1477642801

ISBN-10: 1477642803

DEDICATION

This book is dedicated to:
My beautiful grandchildren who already love reading books.
Keep reading; keep growing!
And…
To my Heavenly Father, from whom and through whom all gifts
have been given, including these beautiful animals from South
Africa in this book and our precious grandchildren.
*"The children of Your servants will continue. And their descendants
will be established before You." Psalm 102:28*

Contents

Dear Grandkids,

Grandpa and I have been in South Africa just a few weeks now. We live on a farm in the valley.

This book shows you some of the wild animals we have seen here. I want you to know about these special animals too. I have some pictures and some stories about when we saw some of them.

Have fun!

Love,
Grandma

PETER THE CHEETAH

The first animal we saw was Peter the **Cheetah**. He is 12 years old. He is very old for a cheetah.

He has yellow fur with black dots. There is a line of black fur that goes from his eye to his mouth. This is a special mark cheetahs have.

He can run very fast. He lives at the Cheetah Reserve near our house.

STRIPED MONGOOSE FAMILY

We saw a family of **striped mongoose** too. Their home is in an old shed in our back yard. They are grey with a black stripe.

They run quickly across our yard every night. They are always with their large family.

Playing and running around are their favorite things to do.

They are lots of fun to watch.

HONEY BADGER

We saw a **honey badger** one day. It lives in the woods near our house also. It ran very fast in front of my little truck. (My small truck is called a *gator*.) It jumped into the bushes to hide.

It has short legs on its black body. A wide white stripe goes from its head to its tail.

It is like the skunk in America.

No, it does not eat honey!

GRASS SNAKE

The next day I was driving home in my gator. I drive on a road of sand and dirt. It is very dusty. It has lots of hills and bumps.

Suddenly, I saw a small **grass snake** in the road! It had a little green stripe on its body.

I ran over the snake! It was not there when I drove by the next time.

I don't think I hurt it.

GUINEA

Guineas are like fat chickens. They are grey with white spots and have something like a red helmet on top. They run, run, run, and then fly away over the fence when we drive by.

One day I heard a strange noise. I saw a group of guineas chasing a cat! They did not want him around.

It was funny to see him running away!

WATERBUCK

One day Grandpa was in the field. It was almost time for supper. He saw a small herd of **waterbucks**.

Maybe they were looking for something to drink. Maybe they were looking for a place to go to bed for the night.

They were brown with a tan circle around their rumps. Many of them also have horns.

STEENBOK

One morning I was driving my gator to work. It was very cold.

A baby **steenbok** ran right in front of me! It ran quickly across the road! I was surprised.

It looked like a small deer. It was light brown with a white belly. It had a short tail with a white tip.

It kicked up the dust and ran very fast. Then it jumped into the bushes to hide.

SNAKE EAGLE

When Grandpa worked in the field he saw many **snake eagles**.

They are like a large American eagle and have dark grey feathers.

As Grandpa plowed the ground, many rats, snakes, and small animals came out of their holes.

The snake eagles flew in the sky to watch for the tiny animals so they could catch them for their supper.

Dear Grandkids,

There are many more animals to see here in South Africa. Some animals that live here you can only see in a zoo in America.

When we see them, I will write to you again. I will have more pictures for you.

Then we can all learn about God's special animals in South Africa together.

Until next time!

Love,
Grandma

QUESTIONS ABOUT THE STORY

1. How old is Peter the Cheetah?
2. What did Grandma run over with her gator?
3. Which two animals ran to hide in the bushes?
4. Why did the small animals come out of their holes to run away?
5. Who lives in the shed with his family?
6. What were the waterbucks looking for?
7. Which animal is like a skunk?
8. What did the guineas chase away?
9. Which animal flies in the sky to watch for his supper?

ANSWERS TO QUESTIONS

1. 12
2. grass snake
3. honey badger and steenbok
4. Grandpa was plowing in the field
5. striped mongoose
6. something to drink or a place to sleep
7. honey badger
8. a cat
9. snake eagle

NEW WORDS FOR YOU?

1. valley
2. pictures
3. cheetah
4. cheetah reserve
5. family
6. striped mongoose
7. honey badger
8. gator
9. America
10. branches
11. different
12. supper
13. waterbucks
14. steenbok
15. surprise
16. eagles
17. feathers
18. together

Africa

South Africa is on the tip of
the continent of Africa.

Dear Grandkids,

I want to show you more new animals here in South Africa. Some ways that I met them are very funny!

In this book you will also hear about my bakkie. This is the pickup truck that Grandpa and I drive here.

Sometimes I also drive my gator. It is like a little truck or an ATV.

Have fun!

Love,
Grandma

MOTHER ZEBRA AND BABY

There are many **zebras** here. They look like striped horses!

We see them when we drive to town. We also see them in the game reserve near our house now. Many of them just arrived in a big truck.

When the truck door opened, they jumped and kicked and ran quickly away. Now they have lots of space to run in their big, new home here.

ROCK MONITOR

My friend came to show me a **rock monitor** today. It looked like a small, green alligator.

He held the rock monitor by the tail. Then he put him on the ground.

Suddenly, the rock monitor ran in my direction! I ran quickly away!

Then he ran into the house! My friend ran to catch him. He took him back to the river.

I was glad.

BLUE LIZARD

I drove the bakkie to our neighbor's house one day. There on the tree was a **blue lizard**.

He was much smaller than the rock monitor. His head was blue, but his body changed colors. His tail was grey.

He sat very quietly. He likes to sit in the sun.

I can not sit very long in the South African sun.

It is too hot for me!

OSTRICH

We have seen many large **ostriches** here in South Africa. Many farmers have them in their fields. When we drive by, we can see them.

They are very tall. Their long legs make them look funny. They have a fat body. It has big, fluffy, dark grey feathers.

They can run fast, but not as fast as a CHEETAH!

MOTHER GIRAFFE AND BABY

We were driving in our bakkie. Suddenly, we saw two **giraffes**! They were eating tree leaves.

One was very tall. The other one was a baby. They both had short beige fur and beautiful brown spots.

We told the others in the bakkie to look!

We went too fast to take a picture.

Maybe next time!

AFRICAN WARTHOG AND BABY

Grandpa was planting corn today. He saw a group of five **warthogs**. They walked across the field.

They look a lot like pigs. They are fat and dark grey.

They live in big holes in the ground. There are big piles of dirt beside their holes. Their homes are easy to find. We see many of them in the fields and by the road.

VERVET MONKEY AND BABY

I drove my bakkie to the store. On the way home I saw a **vervet monkey** run across the road!

He ran to a tree. His friends were there. They sat on the branches waiting.

They were all grey. They had dark faces.

Later I saw many monkeys in a field. They were looking for food.

Yes, they eat bananas too!

ELEPHANT MOTHER AND BABY

Today was very exciting! We went on a "game drive." We took a trip in an open truck with high seats. We looked for big South African animals.

We saw a mother **elephant** drinking water from a small pond. Her baby drank also.

There were 18 elephants nearby rolling in the mud! They were grey, huge, and very tall. One of the young elephants even made a trumpet sound for us!

Dear Grandkids,

Did you see any animals here that you've never seen before? There are many different animals to see here in South Africa. They are God's special creations.

Some animals are endangered. That means there are not many of them alive in the whole earth today.

I'm glad we can enjoy them together.

Until next time!

Love,
Grandma

QUESTIONS ABOUT THE STORY

1. Which animal likes to sit in the sun?
2. Which animal eats bananas?
3. What does Grandma drive to work?
4. Whose friends were waiting for him in the tree?
5. What were the elephants doing?
6. Where did the rock monitor run?
7. Which animals came in a truck?
8. Which animals were rolling in the mud?
9. Which animal did Grandma run away from?
10. Which animal has fluffy grey feathers?

ANSWERS TO QUESTIONS

1. blue lizard
2. monkey
3. gator
4. vervet monkey
5. drinking water; rolling in the mud
6. towards Grandma and into the house
7. zebras
8. elephants
9. rock monitor
10. ostrich

NEW WORDS FOR YOU?

1. bakkie
2. gator
3. zebra
4. striped
5. reserve
6. rock monitor
7. alligator
8. ground
9. direction
10. giraffe
11. beige
12. branches
13. suddenly
14. exciting
15. endangered
16. together